NFL TODAY

THE STORY OF THE
NEW ORLEANS SAINTS

NFL
TODAY

THE STORY OF THE
NEW ORLEANS SAINTS

SARA GILBERT

CREATIVE EDUCATION

Cover: Quarterback Archie Manning (top), Saints
defense, 2008 (bottom)
Page 2: Running back Reggie Bush
Pages 4–5: Louisiana Superdome
Pages 6–7: Quarterback Drew Brees

....

Published by Creative Education
P.O. Box 227, Mankato, Minnesota 56002
Creative Education is an imprint of
The Creative Company
www.thecreativecompany.us

Design and production by Blue Design
Design Associate: Sarah Yakawonis
Printed in the United States of America

Photographs by Corbis (Tami Chappell/Reuters),
Getty Images (Scott Boehm, Stephen Dunn, James
Flores/NFL, George Gojkovich, Chris Graythen, Otto
Greule Jr, Jim Gund, Andy Hayt, Harry How/Allsport,
Nick Laham, Andy Lyons, Ed Mahan/NFL Photos,
Ronald Martinez/Allsport, Al Messerschmidt, Al
Messerschmidt/NFL, NFL Photos, Peter Read Miller/
Sports Illustrated, Tim Sloan/AFP, Jamie Squire/
Allsport, Allen Steele/Allsport, Manny Rubio/NFL
Photos, Mario Tama, Greg Trott, Tyrone Turner/
National Geographic, Lou Witt/NFL)

Library of Congress Cataloging-in-Publication Data

Gilbert, Sara.
The story of the New Orleans Saints / by Sara
Gilbert.
p. cm. — (NFL today)
Includes index.
ISBN 978-1-58341-764-5
1. New Orleans Saints (Football team)—History—
Juvenile literature. I. Title. II. Series.

GV956.N366G55 2009
796.332'640976335—dc22   2008022695

First Edition
9 8 7 6 5 4 3 2 1

CONTENTS

ON THE SIDELINES

MEET THE SAINTS

AN UN-SAINTLY START

X The French Quarter, the oldest and most famous neighborhood in New Orleans, is a popular tourist area characterized by its narrow streets and ornate buildings and balconies.

From the day it was founded by French explorers and fur traders in 1718, New Orleans, Louisiana, has had a reputation as a rough-and-tumble town. It was home to deported slaves, gold miners, and animal trappers whose unruly behavior became a lasting legend for the Southern city. By the time New Orleans was sold to the United States as part of the Louisiana Purchase in 1803, its reputation as a lawless, fun-loving city was firmly established.

Since then, New Orleans has tamed down just enough to become one of the most important cities in the South. It is famous for its annual Mardi Gras celebration, a holdover from its French roots, and as the birthplace of jazz music. It is also known for the National Football League (NFL) franchise that marched into town in 1967: the New Orleans Saints, named for the beloved jazz anthem "When the Saints Go Marching In."

Coach Tom Fears took the reins of the first Saints team knowing that he would be working with a ragtag roster. He had aging castoffs from other teams who were injury-prone and past their prime, as well as inexperienced rookies hoping for a break. At one end of the spectrum was punishing defensive end Doug Atkins, a 6-foot-8 and 257-pound giant who had already logged 14 seasons in the NFL; at the other end was scrappy receiver Danny Abramowicz, who refused to give Fears any reason to cut him during training camp. When receiver John Gilliam returned the opening kickoff of the Saints' first game 94 yards for a touchdown, it seemed that the team might have a chance. In spite of that promising start, the Saints lost not only that game but also the next six and went on to finish their inaugural season 3–11.

Neither the Saints nor their fans were too disappointed, though. In its first few years of existence, the team cobbled together a better record than any NFL expansion team had before, and several players emerged as stars. Abramowicz was the top receiver in the league in 1969, with 73 catches for 1,015 yards and 7 touchdowns. Kicker Tom Dempsey, who was born without toes on his right foot and wore a custom-made, square-toed shoe, set a team record with four field goals against the New York Giants in November 1969.

But it was what Dempsey did a year later that still stands in the team's record books. With new coach J. D. Roberts

ARCHIE MANNING

QUARTERBACK
SAINTS SEASONS: 1971–82
HEIGHT: 6-FOOT-3
WEIGHT: 212 POUNDS

The New Orleans Saints selected Archie Manning with the second pick of the 1971 NFL Draft. Manning had been a sensational quarterback at the University of Mississippi, and the Saints hoped that his strong, accurate arm would lead them to the top. But although Manning's impressive 11-year career with the Saints included two trips to the Pro Bowl and Player of the Year honors in 1978, it never once included a winning season. Among Manning's statistical achievements with the Saints—such as his 21,734 passing yards and 115 touchdowns—is an even more telling number: 340 sacks. Manning played behind an offensive line that struggled to protect the quarterback, which left him flat on his back at the end of many plays. Manning played with the Houston Oilers and the Minnesota Vikings after the Saints traded him away in 1982, but he returned to New Orleans to raise his family— including sons Peyton and Eli, who both followed in their father's footsteps as quarterbacks in the NFL—after retirement. Today, he serves as an analyst with the Saints' radio and preseason television broadcasts.

[11]

ON THE SIDELINES

NAMING THE SAINTS

From the day in 1962 that New Orleans businessman Dave Dixon began campaigning for an NFL team in his hometown, he knew exactly what it should be called: the New Orleans Saints, in honor of the popular tune that New Orleans jazz legend Louis Armstrong had made famous in the 1930s. He was so certain about the team's future name that he had it printed on the pencils that he generously distributed. Although Dixon had made his choice very clear, a local newspaper still decided to run a naming contest when the city was officially awarded a team in 1966. Among the many suggestions received were Deltas, Jazz Kings, Tarpons, Tigers, Nolas, Blues, Domes, and Mudbugs. Dixon overruled each of them. He even cleared his selection with the archbishop of New Orleans. "I told him some gentlemen think somehow or another the name 'Saints' for our football team might be a little sacrilegious," Dixon said. "The archbishop replied, 'It's certainly not sacrilegious. Besides, I have a terrible instinct that we're going to need all the help we can get.'"

prowling the sidelines, Dempsey was sent in to attempt a 63-yard field goal in the waning seconds of a game against the Detroit Lions. When his record-setting kick sailed through the uprights, and the Saints won 19–17, the players hoisted their coach up in celebration. "They carried J. D. off the field like he was a hero," said Peter Finney, a longtime New Orleans newpaperman. "J. D. was on top of the world."

Unfortunately, that was as good as it would get for the Saints under Roberts. The team lost the final six games of the 1970 season to end with a 2–11–1 record and tallied only six more wins in the following two seasons. Roberts was fired before the start of the 1973 season. But by then, there was a new savior in the Saints' sights: quarterback Archie Manning, who had gone to the Saints with the second overall pick of the 1971 NFL Draft. Manning was a complete athlete who could run almost as well as he could throw, and the Saints pinned their hopes for success on him.

In Manning's first game of the 1971 season, the Saints faced the Los Angeles Rams, a team New Orleans had never beaten. Manning passed for one touchdown and ran for another on the final play of the game to seal a 24–20 Saints victory. That game would set the tone for his career. During his 11 seasons in New Orleans, the scrappy quarterback would

play in two Pro Bowls and set virtually every team passing record. But no matter how talented he was, Manning couldn't guide the Saints to a winning record by himself.

New coach Hank Stram tried to find some help for his quarterback. In the 1976 NFL Draft, the Saints used their top two choices to select fleet-footed running backs Chuck Muncie and Tony Galbreath. Muncie set a club record with 811 rushing yards in 1977, and Galbreath led the team in carries per game with 14 that same year, but the Saints remained mired at the bottom of the National Football Conference (NFC) West Division standings with a 4–10 record in 1976 and a 3–11 mark in 1977.

Things changed for the better in 1978. That year, Manning threw for 3,416 yards and was honored as the NFC's Player of the Year, while the Saints assembled their finest season yet, posting 7 wins and 9 losses. In 1979, Muncie ran wild, becoming the first Saints player to collect more than 1,000 rushing yards in a season when he finished with 1,198 yards. That same year, speedy young receiver Wes Chandler set a club record with 1,069 receiving yards. The team finally broke even with an 8–8 record. "We're going to be there very soon," linebacker Joe Federspiel told reporters. "This town is dying for a winner, and everyone on this team is dying to be one."

TOM BENSON

TEAM OWNER
SAINTS SEASONS: 1985–PRESENT

Tom Benson made his fortune selling cars. The New Orleans native owned several successful automobile dealerships in Louisiana and Texas, which allowed the savvy businessman to invest in a network of local banks. But it was his multimillion-dollar investment in the New Orleans Saints that made Benson famous. In 1985, as rumors circulated that out-of-state buyers might be trying to move the team elsewhere, Benson bought the Saints from original owner John Mecom. Benson's colorful character and love for his hometown team were soon made obvious to both the players and their fans, who enjoyed the Saints' first winning season just two years after he took over. Benson's popularity began to fade in 2001, however, when he threatened to move the team to San Antonio, where his businesses were headquartered. That possibility resurfaced in 2005, when the Louisiana Superdome was damaged by Hurricane Katrina, and the Saints were forced to play several games in San Antonio. However, Benson publicly pledged his support to New Orleans and committed both himself and the team to helping the city recover.

SAINTS OR AIN'TS?

Despite the momentum they had been building, the Saints' hopes were dashed during the 1980 season. The defense collapsed completely, and the team lost its first 14 games, many by wide margins. The offense also sputtered after Muncie, who had been honored as the Most Valuable Player (MVP) of the Pro Bowl in January, was traded away in October. As both fans and newspaper writers began calling the team the "Ain'ts," coach Dick Nolan was fired—the sixth coach to be dismissed in the Saints' 13-year history. By season's end, the team had filed its worst record yet: 1–15.

The 1981 season started with a new leader, former Houston Oilers coach O. A. "Bum" Phillips, and sensational new running back George Rogers. Rogers had won the 1980 Heisman Trophy as the best college player in the country while attending the University of South Carolina, and the Saints snatched him up in the 1981 NFL Draft. In his rookie year, Rogers led the league in rushing with a jaw-dropping 1,674 yards and was an easy choice as NFL Rookie of the Year.

Phillips was rewarded with a promotion to general manager in 1982, but to the dismay of the Saints' faithful fans, his first order of business was to trade Manning to the Oilers for tackle Leon Gray. Manning had grown up with the team and had taken it to the cusp of competitiveness, but

X One of the first Saints standouts, Chuck Muncie (right) was a 230-pound bruiser who often surprised opposing defenses with his elusive running moves and soft hands as a receiver.

Phillips believed that a stronger defensive line was what the team needed now. "It broke my heart to leave the Saints," Manning said. "I don't think it had to do with Bum disliking me. I think he had a quick-fix agenda and just wanted to win right away, with his guys."

Phillips and the Saints won four games during the strike-shortened 1982 season. The next year began with Rogers breaking Chuck Muncie's single-game rushing total by racing for 206 yards in a 28–17 victory over the St. Louis Cardinals. That was the first of eight wins for the Saints. Unfortunately, the season ended with the Saints just outside the playoffs, when the Los Angeles Rams kicked a game-winning field goal with six seconds left in the last game of the season. Although the Saints had yet to record a winning season, optimism was running high once again.

Defensively, New Orleans was fielding a fine team by this time. The defense, anchored by linemen Derland Moore, Jim Wilks, Frank Warren, and Bruce Clark, led the league in pass defense throughout 1983 and 1984. But offensively, there were holes to fill. Management had tried to plug these holes with time-tested veterans, including quarterback Ken Stabler and running back Earl Campbell, both of whom had played for Phillips in Houston. But both were in the twilight

X Big defensive end Frank Warren spent his entire 13-season NFL career in a New Orleans uniform, notching 52.5 quarterback sacks.

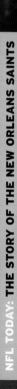

ON THE SIDELINES

FRUSTRATED FANS

New Orleans Saints fans were used to losing. By the time the 1980 season started, the Saints had lost more than 125 games in 13 years. But after five consecutive losses in 1980, even stoic Saints fans were embarrassed— especially Bobby LeCompte, a local bar manager who still attended each dreadful home game. Because anyone who recognized him teased him about his loyalty to the team, he decided to hide his face at the games. He cut ear, eye, nose, and mouth holes in a paper bag, placed a Saints sticker on it, and scrawled the word "Ain'ts" across it. He and a few friends wore these bags over their heads as New Orleans lost to the Atlanta Falcons on October 19. The next week, more fans showed up wearing bags. By the time the 0–11 Saints played the Los Angeles Rams on Monday Night Football in November, the Superdome was full of decorated bags. Despite team attempts to ban the bags, fans continued to wear them during the dismal 1–15 season, and the idea spread to fans of other failing teams as well.

of their careers, and neither could offer the kind of offensive spark the team needed.

The spark New Orleans needed came in the form of a new owner. John W. Mecom Jr., leader of the original ownership group, had officially put the team on the market late in 1984. On May 31, 1985, New Orleans businessman Tom Benson paid more than $70 million for the Saints. And then he spent even more money in overhauling the organization from top to bottom, including hiring a new general manager and

Although New Orleans was mediocre in the mid-1980s, its defense put on some great shows; in 1983 and 1984, the Saints were the NFL's top-ranked defense against the pass. X

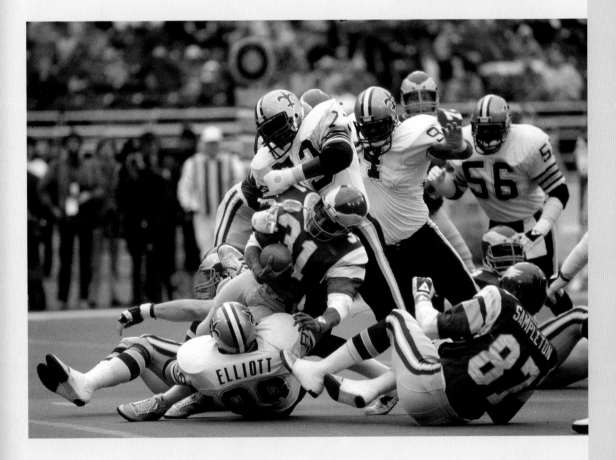

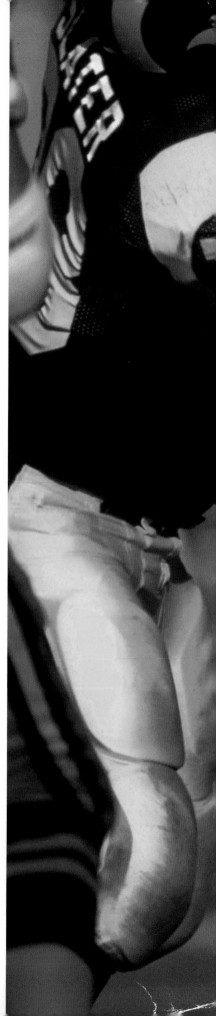

X Rickey Jackson had a nose for the ball; the tenacious linebacker, who represented the Saints in 6 Pro Bowls, recovered a whopping 29 fumbles during the course of his career.

replacing much of the front office staff. He even tried to change the team's gold and black uniforms to blue and gold—but backed off after the results of a poll showed that fans didn't like the idea.

Howemer, the fans did like the first head coach under Benson's watch: Jim Mora took over in 1986 and immediately started fining, benching, and cutting players until he found the right combination of players to put on the field. Mora's sole focus was to turn the "Ain'ts" into winners. So, during the sweltering Louisiana summer, he put the squad to the test, running post-practice sprints until players collapsed from the heat. "I had never trained a team in that kind of heat before. I was going to make an impression," he said later. "The big guys were dying out there on us. I never really noticed."

What Mora and Saints fans did notice was a new toughness to the team. Two decades after the Saints began play, all the pieces were finally falling into place. Rookie running back Rueben Mays ran nonstop in 1986, setting team records and earning NFL Rookie of the Year honors along the way. Kicker Morten Andersen and linebacker Rickey Jackson joined him at the annual Pro Bowl in Hawaii. But while the Saints' 7–9 record was an improvement, it wasn't quite what the team or its fans were hoping for.

WINNING WAYS

The 1987 season did not start promisingly. An NFL players' strike cancelled one game and forced teams to play with replacement players for three games. When the regular roster returned on October 25, the Saints were topped by the San Francisco 49ers in a 24–22 thriller that inspired Coach Mora's infamous "coulda, woulda, shoulda" speech about how his team just wasn't good enough to win. His emotional outburst triggered a response in the players. "I think that was something that shook the guys and woke everybody up," said linebacker Sam Mills. "It made the guys think, 'Hey, we've gotta get the ball rolling.'"

So they did. The very next Sunday, the Saints routed their rivals, the Atlanta Falcons, 38–0. That victory launched an unprecedented winning streak that lasted for the remaining eight games of the season. When New Orleans' bruising defense made two impressive stops of the charging Pittsburgh Steelers offense late in a game at the end of November to win 20–16, the Saints achieved what had so far

Quarterback Bobby Hebert earned a place in the Saints' history books by leading New Orleans to its first playoff berth; he was inducted into the Saints Hall of Fame in 1999. **X**

SAM MILLS

LINEBACKER
SAINTS SEASONS: 1986–94
HEIGHT: 5-FOOT-9
WEIGHT: 229 POUNDS

Sam Mills was told that he was too small to play in the NFL. And when compared with most other linebackers, Mills certainly appeared tiny. But he was tough, tenacious, and had surprising speed for his size—qualities that served him well during his 12-year professional career and earned him the nickname "The Field Mouse." Mills anchored the Saints' defense for the better part of a decade, earning four selections to the Pro Bowl along the way. Saints coach Jim Mora, who first worked with the linebacker in the United States Football League, credited Mills's strong work ethic as what made him one of the best players he'd ever coached. When Mora moved to New Orleans, Mills followed him. In the preseason of 2003, Mills, then a linebackers coach for the Carolina Panthers, was diagnosed with intestinal cancer. He died at his home in Charlotte, North Carolina, in 2005, at the age of 45. "He never backed away from a battle and took on each and every challenge with the heart of a champion," a spokesperson for the Saints said in a tribute to Mills.

been unattainable in their history: a winning record. The next week, a victory over the Tampa Bay Buccaneers guaranteed another first: a trip to the playoffs. With an incredible 12–3 record in hand, the Saints marched triumphantly into the Wild Card game against the Minnesota Vikings, only to lose 44–10.

Despite that defeat, the sweet smell of success lingered in New Orleans, as Mora was named NFL Coach of the Year and six Saints players were selected as Pro-Bowlers. The late 1980s were characterized by a defense that effectively shut down its opponents with the help of nimble but tough linebackers such as Mills, Jackson, and Pat Swilling rushing opposing quarterbacks, tackling, and forcing fumbles. And in scrappy young quarterback Bobby "The Cajun Cannon" Hebert, the team had finally found a suitable replacement for Archie Manning. Between Hebert's strong right arm and Andersen's powerful left leg, the offense was setting new team scoring records.

The Saints remained near the top of the NFC standings in the seasons that followed, making the playoffs again in 1990, 1991, and 1992. At one point in 1991, New Orleans sat atop the NFC West with an incredible 9–1 record and a five-game lead over the 49ers. "Nine and one is beautiful," Mills remarked, "but we still have a ways to go."

THE BENSON BOOGIE

Tom Benson couldn't help himself. The new owner of the New Orleans Saints had left his luxury suite in the Louisiana Superdome to head down to the field to celebrate the team's rout of the Tampa Bay Buccaneers on October 19, 1986. He was too busy shaking hands and slapping shoulders to notice that there were still six minutes left on the clock. He just kept congratulating players and coaches, and finally, he did a happy little dance that ended up being pictured in the newspaper the next day. Benson did the same dance when the Saints beat the San Francisco 49ers a few weeks later, and again when they topped the Los Angeles Rams in a close 6–0 game. By then, his dance had a name: "The Benson Boogie." Fans began encouraging the owner to dance, and Benson has boogied on the sidelines every time the Saints win at home since then. "That started with a lot of enthusiasm, something between me and the fans," Benson said. "I've told friends that if we win the Super Bowl, you'll see me out there."

Pat Swilling (pictured), Rickey Jackson, Sam Mills, and Vaughn Johnson made up "The Dome Patrol," a linebacker quartet that was the NFL's most fearsome in the early 1990s. **X**

Mills' guarded optimism reflected what everyone in the Saints organization seemed to know: There was still a monkey on the Saints' backs. Every time they made it to the playoffs, they fell in the first round. The Chicago Bears beat them 16–6 in 1990. Then the Atlanta Falcons came from behind in the 1991 Wild Card game to win 27–20. In 1992, the Philadelphia

JIM MORA

COACH
SAINTS SEASONS: 1986-96

Jim Mora's career with the Saints was an emotional roller coaster. He took the reins of a team that had never recorded a winning season and led it to a 12–3 record in only his second season at the helm. The Saints finished at .500 or better seven times under Mora and made it to the playoffs four times. But Mora, who was honored as the NFL Coach of the Year in 1987, often let his temper get the best of him. His emotional postgame press conferences were often laced with profanity, including the famous "coulda, woulda, shoulda" speech that preceded the Saints' nine-game winning streak in 1987. He's also remembered for launching into a tirade after the Saints were beaten by the Carolina Panthers midway through the 1996 season—and for abruptly resigning shortly thereafter. From 1998 through 2001, Mora coached the Indianapolis Colts. At the time of his retirement from the NFL in 2001, he had compiled a career coaching record of 125–112. Ninety-three of those wins were with the Saints.

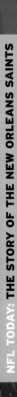
ON THE SIDELINES

A SAINTLY SPEECH

Jim Mora didn't walk into the postgame press conference on October 25, 1987, with a script in hand. All the New Orleans coach had was the memory of his team's bitter defeat that day, a 24–22 loss to the mighty San Francisco 49ers that sent the Saints' record to 3–3. But that was enough to spur one of the most motivational speeches in football history. "The Saints ain't good enough," Mora fumed. "It's that simple." He called the team "the worst franchise in the history of the National Football League" and could barely describe how upset he was. "I'm sick of coulda, woulda, shoulda, coming close, if only," he said. It wasn't just the reporters who were listening, however. His players heard every word as well—and they took it to heart. The Saints won their next nine games and ended the season with a winning record, the first time that had ever happened for New Orleans. "That's exactly what we needed," quarterback Bobby Hebert said. "The team needed a Mora personality. He gave us that speech, and we won nine straight games."

Eagles scored 29 points in the fourth quarter to overcome a 20–7 deficit and defeat the Saints 36–20.

Then, just as suddenly as the Saints had risen, they slid back down in the standings. After posting a 12–4 record in 1992, the Saints dropped to 8–8 in 1993. The next two years, they posted 7–9 records and disappeared from the playoff picture. As the face of the Saints changed—with Swilling being traded for first-round draft pick tackle Willie Roaf, Hebert being replaced by veteran quarterback Jim Everett, and Andersen being released—so did the team's fortunes. The bottom fell out in 1996, when the Saints posted only two wins in the first half of the season.

That was the last straw for Coach Mora. On October 20, 1996, after his team suffered a 19–7 loss to the Carolina Panthers, the Saints' coach erupted in a postgame press conference that was punctuated with profanity. "It was an awful performance by our football team," he said. "We should be totally embarrassed, totally ashamed." That night, Mora called Benson and gave his immediate resignation.

STARS AND STORMS

X --------

The 1997 Saints strutted into the Superdome with a bold new coach, "Iron" Mike Ditka, who had led the 1985 Chicago Bears to victory in Super Bowl XX. His hiring boosted season-ticket sales, but it didn't lift the morale of the sagging Saints. Ditka shuffled players in and out of starting roles throughout the 1997 season. He used no fewer than four quarterbacks, including former Heisman Trophy winner Danny Wuerffel.

The Saints' defense was one of the best in the league, but the inconsistent offense sputtered. New Orleans posted 6–10 records in both 1997 and 1998, in third place in the NFC West and out of playoff contention. Ditka's solution was to trade eight draft picks to the Washington Redskins for the opportunity to select University of Texas running back Ricky Williams fifth overall in the 1999 NFL Draft.

Williams had been a superstar in college, rushing for 2,124 yards in his final season and winning the Heisman Trophy. Unfortunately, he had too many problems of his own to be able to solve all the Saints' struggles. Williams would battle injuries and personal problems in his three seasons with New Orleans

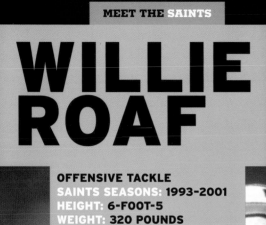

WILLIE ROAF

OFFENSIVE TACKLE
SAINTS SEASONS: 1993-2001
HEIGHT: 6-FOOT-5
WEIGHT: 320 POUNDS

NFL TODAY: THE STORY OF THE NEW ORLEANS SAINTS

In seven of the nine seasons that Willie Roaf played for the New Orleans Saints, the hulking offensive lineman earned a place in the Pro Bowl—and he went four more times as a member of the Kansas City Chiefs. That kind of play is exactly what the Saints were hoping for when they drafted Roaf with the eighth overall pick of the 1993 NFL Draft. He had enjoyed an outstanding college football career at Louisiana Tech, developing the strength and quickness that would define his professional career as well. Roaf became one of the best offensive linemen in the game and was a cornerstone of the Saints' offense. Unfortunately, in the middle of the 2001 season, Roaf publicly demanded to be traded, citing irreconcilable differences with new coach Jim Haslett as the reason. He was dealt to the Kansas City Chiefs during the off-season, where he played for four more years and was a valuable asset to the offense once again. Two years after his retirement in 2006, Roaf was inducted into the Saints Hall of Fame.

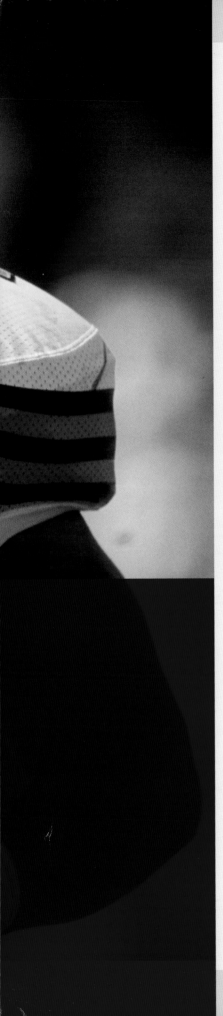

and eventually be traded to Miami. As the team stumbled

through a 3–13 season in 1999, owner Tom Benson promised that

the next season would be different. "I will take whatever steps

necessary to make the New Orleans Saints a winning franchise,"

he said.

Benson's first step was to fire Ditka and hire coach Jim

Haslett. Then the Saints traded for Aaron Brooks, a nimble

young quarterback who had been Brett Favre's backup with

the Green Bay Packers. Brooks connected with speedy receiver

Joe Horn a club-record 94 times in 2000 as the resurgent

Saints claimed first place in the NFC West and returned to the

playoffs after a seven-year absence.

X Although known as "The Texas Tornado" during his sensational college career, running back Ricky Williams showed only glimpses of brilliance during his three years with the Saints.

X Brash receiver Joe Horn posted more than 1,000 receiving yards in 4 different seasons, including 2004, when he set new Saints records with 1,399 yards and 11 touchdowns.

The Saints met the defending Super Bowl champion St. Louis Rams in the Wild Card game. Brooks threw four touchdown passes, including three to reliable receiver Willie Jackson, but it was special teams man Brian Milne who sealed the Saints' first-ever playoff victory. With the Saints up by three points and less than two minutes remaining, Rams receiver Az-Zahir Hakim called for a fair catch of a New Orleans punt—but the ball bounced out of his hands. Milne picked it up, eliminating St. Louis's last chance to score. Even though the Saints lost to the Minnesota Vikings a week later,

THE DREADLOCK DUO

Mike Ditka was so sure that running back Ricky Williams would save the Saints that he traded an unprecedented eight draft picks to land Williams in the 1999 NFL Draft. To welcome Williams to New Orleans the day after the draft, Ditka scheduled a press conference and an autograph session with fans. When Williams, who wore his hair in short, tight dreadlocks, stepped in front of the media, Ditka joined him, wearing a wig with long, black dreadlocks. As 1,500 fans lined up to get autographs, Ditka took the microphone to make a bold proclamation. "We're going to win the Super Bowl," he said. "And I'm not talking about 10 years from now either, gang. Now is the future. We got Ricky, and he's going to be the final piece in the puzzle. I really believe that." *ESPN The Magazine* had Ditka and Williams pose for a cover dressed as a bride and groom with the headline, "For Better or Worse." But that vow would not hold true, as Ditka was fired by the end of the season, and Williams was traded three years later.

REGGIE BUSH

RUNNING BACK
SAINTS SEASONS: 2006-PRESENT
HEIGHT: 6 FEET
WEIGHT: 200 POUNDS

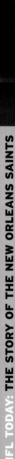

Most people expected Reggie Bush to be taken with the first overall pick in the 2006 NFL Draft. But if he had been, the Heisman Trophy winner who had been hyped up by football experts and analysts since deciding to forego his senior year to turn pro would have gone to the Houston Texans. When the Texans decided to take a defensive end instead, the Saints were able to select Bush with the second pick. Within a week, more than 15,000 Reggie Bush jerseys had been ordered by eager fans, even though his official number had not yet been decided. Unfortunately, Bush's rookie season wasn't as phenomenal as fans had hoped (he recorded an unremarkable 565 rushing yards and 6 touchdowns), and injuries slowed his progress in 2007. But he did establish himself as a star off the field: Bush has appeared in music videos and television commercials, including advertisements for the video game *Madden NFL 08*. Before the start of the 2008 season, Bush returned his focus to football, saying, "I'm just trying to find every edge possible to get better."

New Orleans had finally tasted victory in the postseason, and the team was hungry for more.

But the Saints missed the playoffs the following season, finishing 7–9 and in third place in the division. It was the same story in 2002, even with spirited running back Deuce McAllister eating up more than 100 yards in 8 different games. In fact, despite terrific seasons by Brooks, McAllister, and kicker John Carney, the Saints remained out of playoff contention in both 2003 and 2004 as well.

T hen, in 2005, football became an afterthought for most of Louisiana. On August 29, Hurricane Katrina devastated New Orleans and much of the Gulf Coast region. The Louisiana Superdome, the Saints' home since 1975, became an emergency shelter for thousands of residents

X Despite going undrafted out of college, reliable safety Jay Bellamy found work in the NFL for 14 years—7 of them in New Orleans.

whose homes were either underwater or torn to pieces. The displaced Saints shuttled between Tiger Stadium at Louisiana State University and the Alamodome in San Antonio, Texas, for their home games and managed only three wins in the chaotic season that ensued.

The bright spot in the Saints' string of bad luck was securing the second overall pick in the 2006 NFL Draft, with which the team selected swift running back Reggie Bush. Bush was in the backfield when the Saints returned to the Superdome for a Monday Night Football game on September 25, 2006. Sparked by the energetic response of fans in their recovering home city and the arm of new quarterback Drew Brees, the Saints won that night and kept winning to finish 10–6 and in first place in the NFC South Division (which was created after the NFL expanded in 2002). After winning the first playoff game against the Philadelphia Eagles, the Saints fell in the NFC Championship Game to the Chicago Bears.

The Saints remained contenders in 2007 and 2008 but could not reach the postseason again. Still, they were exciting to watch. Linebacker Scott Fujita led the defense, while coach Sean Payton directed a high-powered passing offense starring Brees, Bush, and such up-and-comers as receiver Lance Moore.

ROAD TO RECOVERY

When Hurricane Katrina surged through New Orleans on August 29, 2005, it left more than 250,000 of the city's 450,000 residents stranded. Among those were many Saints players, executives, and front office staff members, who also had to rebuild homes and lives that had been disrupted by the storm. The Saints invested $185.4 million, $20 million of which came in the form of grants from the NFL, in renovating the Louisiana Superdome, which had been damaged by the storm and further ruined when almost 30,000 evacuees had to take shelter there for 6 days. But rebuilding was just one step in the healing process. For many people in New Orleans and throughout the U.S., football became an important part of the recovery process. Fans were ready and waiting when the team returned to New Orleans in 2006. In the months leading up to the start of the 2006 season, the Saints' management announced that they had sold a franchise record of 54,969 season tickets. "We all need to be entertained," one new season-ticket holder said. "We're all on the comeback trail together."

X With an offense led by Drew Brees (number 9), who passed for an incredible 5,069 yards in 2008, the Saints found a sunny forecast after Hurricane Katrina.

X A 330-pound run-stopping specialist, tackle Hollis Thomas became an important anchor on the Saints' defensive line after New Orleans traded for him in 2006.

X A seventh-round draft pick in 2006, receiver Marques Colston surprised the league by catching 168 passes in his first 2 seasons, setting a new NFL record.

It may have taken the New Orleans Saints 21 years to record their first winning season, but their fans never gave up on them. And in a city that has survived both its wild beginnings and the worst weather imaginable, those fans aren't likely to give up hope anytime soon. When the Saints finally do bring home a Super Bowl trophy, there will undoubtedly be a big party in New Orleans, a city that knows how to celebrate.

INDEX